D1398552

coffee

discovering, exploring, enjoying

coffee

discovering, exploring, enjoying

hattie ellis

photography by debi treloar

RYLAND
PETERS
& SMALL
LONDON NEW YORK

*To Clare Moberly, who at the time of writing
drinks the brew in Brazil.*

Designer Luis Peral-Aranda
Senior Editor Sophie Bevan
Picture Research Manager Kate Brunt
Production Tamsin Curwood
Art Director Gabriella Le Grazie
Publishing Director Alison Starling

Stylist Emily Chalmers
Food Stylist Fiona Smith

First published in the United States in 2002
by Ryland Peters & Small, Inc
519 Broadway, 5th Floor
New York, NY 10012
www.rylandpeters.com

10 9 8 7 6 5 4 3 2

Library of Congress Cataloging-in-Publication Data

Ellis, Hattie.
    Coffee : discovering, exploring, enjoying / Hattie Ellis ;
photograph by Debi Trelor.
        p. cm.
    Includes index.
    ISBN 1 84172 349 5
    1. Coffee brewing. 2. Coffee. I. Title.

TX817.C6 E43 2002
641.6`373--dc21
                                        2002024851

Printed and bound in China

contents

what is coffee?

Coffee beans are the seeds inside the cherries of an evergreen plant that grows in the humid lands between the tropic of Cancer and the tropic of Capricorn. After the cherries are harvested and processed to remove the outer layers, the green beans travel around the world. Roasted, ground, and mixed with hot water, their concentrated, aromatic flavors are released to make one of the most remarkable and celebrated drinks in the world. Utterly transformed from plant to cup, the tastes—of lemon, of blueberries, of wine—that lie within this bitter black brew can still remind you of its origins at the heart of a fruit.

Ancient as tribes and irrepressibly modern, coffee adapts itself to time and place, encompassing the romantic, the industrious, and the day-to-day. Its dynamic history is full of tales of passion and intrigue, yet it is also the drink of breakfast and of mid-morning office breaks. Prized for its intriguing range of flavors and styles, used as a digestive, relied upon as a stimulant, coffee excites and focuses the brain along with the rest of the body. It brings us together over cups and conversation. Its aromatic allure can beckon us away from our daily business to a café for a quiet sip, a newspaper, and a view of the world. Solitary or sociable, it allows us both to unwind and to recharge.

The current surge of interest in coffee has developed through a growing awareness of the quality end of the market, in freshly roasted beans that have a particular provenance and a distinctive taste, and in the many ways of drinking coffee, such as cappuccino and espresso. This book celebrates coffee in all its forms and looks at how to discover and enjoy its many flavors and possibilities.

The outer layers of the cherries from the coffee plant are removed (above and opposite, below right) to get the green beans. These can be transported around the world and are then roasted, ground, and added to hot water to make coffee.

Coffee drinking began in Ethiopia and spread to Arabia and the Islamic world before traveling around the rest of the globe. The black brew stirred up a storm of interest wherever it went, as people took to this new drink with its remarkable ability to awake and refresh both mind and body.

the buzz

the origins of coffee

Ethiopia, believed by many to be the ancient birthplace of mankind, is where coffee's long history begins. Legend tells of a goatherd in Abyssinia called Kaldi who noticed his animals prancing around after nibbling at the leaves and fruit of particular bushes. So it was that, right from the start, the plant was recognized and prized as a stimulant. Monks took coffee to keep them awake for nocturnal prayers, and travelers rolled the cherries with fat into balls to make an early trail food.

Coffea arabica was cultivated by the Arabs, who used coffee as both a medicine and as a pleasurable stimulant. Coffeehouses sprang up where people would meet to drink, play backgammon, talk, and listen to music and storytelling. Pilgrims and traders spread the bean around the Muslim world, and its fame—and consumption—spanned North Africa, Turkey, and Persia.

Although coffee was initially prized by the religious, the coffeehouses came to be regarded as subversive—as places of temptation and ideological ferment—and the early history of coffee is full of stories of suppression. Yet its progress around the world was indefatigable, as people discovered this *qahwa al-bon*, "wine of the bean," that could waken mind, spirit, and senses.

spread around the world

Coffee consumption really took off in the West from the 17th century on. One of the bean's earliest European destinations was the trade center of Venice, which received coffee with other goods from the East. At first, Italian Christian leaders rejected the drink as darkly satanic and wanted it excommunicated. But Pope Clement VIII took a sip, realized this delectable taste was here to stay, and blessed the new brew as heavenly instead.

Bags of green beans were left behind by the Turks, who had besieged Vienna in 1683. Franz George Kolschitzky, a Pole who went behind enemy lines for the Austrians, became a double hero when he showed how the beans could be turned into a drink—Viennese coffee and the Viennese café were born.

Coffeehouses popularized the drink wherever it was consumed. Coinciding with the start of newspapers and the thinking of the Enlightenment, coffee became known as "the drink of democracy." British coffeehouses were referred to as "penny universities" because, for the price of a cup of coffee, people could meet, talk, and participate in the political and philosophical discussions of the day. "The history of coffee houses," wrote Isaac D'Israeli, "… was that of the manners, the morals and the politics of a people." These meeting places often attracted specific groups of people; and institutions still in existence today, such as the insurers Lloyds of London, began as coffeehouses.

The first French café, Café Procope, opened its doors opposite the Comédie Française in 1689, and soon became the haunt of philosophers, writers, and political activists. By the end of the 1700s, there were 800 cafés in Paris, and by 1843 there were 3,000.

After the Boston Tea Party, Americans saw tea as "unpatriotic" and became a nation of coffee drinkers. The bean, now grown outside Africa and Arabia, arrived in Latin America, which was to become the biggest producer of coffee in the world, on the doorstep of the booming U.S. market.

coffee trade

Coffee grows on vast Brazilian plantations and is collected from the wild in Ethiopian forests; it is cultivated on the ancient terraces carved into the steep mountainsides of Yemen and on Indonesian smallholdings, where the beans can still be spread out to dry on the roadside. All these beans, and many others besides, make their way into markets, local and global. In volume, coffee is the second most traded commodity in the world, after oil.

Coffee production can be affected by political upheaval, when growers may switch from export crops to subsistence farming, and it is prone to the natural disasters such as frost, earthquakes, hurricanes, and floods that can devastate the tropics. The price fluctuations that affect any global commodity can mean disaster to the small grower, which is why the Fair Trade movement (see page 62) guarantees a stable price that goes directly to the producer and enables them to continue farming in a sustainable way.

Some of the best coffees from around the world end up in specialized coffee suppliers. These professionals, and the wholesalers who supply them, have the skill, the experience, and the contacts to source consistently good beans from the market, tasting each new crop and roasting every batch of beans to perfection to bring out their optimum flavors. They will create and maintain house blends, supply you with your favorite coffees, and enable you to explore a wider range of beans. Follow the tantalizing aroma that wisps out through the door of a good coffee shop or café, and it will lead you to a whole world of flavor.

famous coffee drinkers

Coffee gives people energy, and cafés bring them together—a potent combination that has long whirred the wheels of political, creative, and philosophical revolutions. Voltaire downed as many as 50 cups a day. Beethoven would count 60 beans into a single cup. The writing of Goethe's *Sorrows of Young Werther* was fueled by caffeine. Balzac would walk across Paris to get three kinds of coffee from different shops to make his favored blend that kept him awake to write from midnight until noon. He explained that when he drank coffee, "… ideas begin to move. Things remembered arrive at full gallop … the shafts of wit start up like sharp-shooters. Similes arise, the paper is covered in ink …."

The Boston Tea Party was planned in secrecy at the Green Dragon coffeehouse. And, just a few years later, in 1789, Desmoulins whipped up a revolutionary crowd when he leapt onto a table to speak from the Café Foy in Paris; two days later, the Bastille was stormed.

"Strong coffee, and plenty, awakens me," said Napoleon, who favored a Brazilian Santos-Mocha blend. "It gives me warmth, an unusual force, a pain that is not without pleasure. I would rather suffer than be senseless."

Jean Paul Sartre and Simone de Beauvoir wrote at Les Deux Magots, a quintessential Left Bank café, while the Beat Poets drank coffee and talked the talk at the Caffe Trieste and the Co-Existence Bagel Shop in San Fransisco. Impressionism, Surrealism, Cubism, Existentialism—all these movements brewed in the atmosphere of cafés and coffee shops. Alcohol may incite the passions, but coffee engenders both excitement and action.

You can travel the world in a coffee cup. From fruity Kenyans to chocolatey Guatemalans, from spicy Indonesians to clean Costa Ricans, entrance your taste buds with the host of different roasts, blends, and flavors available.

the beans

understanding terms

The details given on labels, coffee menus, and the lists of specialized retailers indicate the sellers' knowledge of the origin and character of the beans, and will give you some idea of what to expect. Look, for example, for coffees that come from a particular place—be it a single estate or an area—where they take a pride in the distinctiveness and quality of their product.

Arabica beans, from the plant *Coffea arabica*, are the coffee connoisseur's choice. The plant grows best at higher altitudes, and its slowly grown, hard beans have more flavor than coffees from the more easily grown *Coffea robusta* beans. In coffee shops and cafés, also look out for labels stating the coffee is "high grown" or "hard bean."

Older varieties of the arabica coffee plant, such as Bourbon, are well worth seeking out. So, too, are specialties such as Peaberry coffee, which comes from cherries with a single, rounder bean, and the large Maragogype, or "elephant" beans, which are prized for both their appearance and their smooth taste.

The way in which the beans are separated from their surrounding pulp also plays a part in the character of the coffee in your cup. Wet-processed, or washed, beans tend to have lighter, subtle flavors, while the dry-processed beans, from areas where water is in short supply, can have an earthy, fruity character.

When tasting coffee, notice the aroma and the flavors inside the cup; the body, which is the feel of the coffee in your mouth, cleanly light to lusciously full; and its acidity, which spreads across your tongue and lifts the drink by providing an additional, lively layer of enjoyment.

OPPOSITE, CLOCKWISE FROM TOP LEFT Freshly ground coffee; Colombian beans; very dark roasted beans; green beans; Kibo Chagga beans from Tanzania; Middle Eastern coffee with cardamom seeds.

roasts and blends

Coffee is exported as green beans. These are sent around the world in sacks, and are then roasted by specialists to bring out their subtle flavors. As the beans heat up and turn glossy brown, the oils develop that are the secret of their marvelous flavor.

Roasts vary from light brown through medium to the very dark beans favored by the French and Italians. Light roasts, such as "cinnamon," have a more delicate, mildly aromatic taste. Medium roasts, also known as "city" or "American," are slightly stronger. Viennese roasts are a little darker than medium, while French, Italian, and Continental roasts edge into deep brown and near-black, producing enticingly bitter, richly pungent flavors such as those found in espresso.

The art of blending is to marry different beans together to create a harmonious balance of flavors, acidity, and body. Specialized coffee suppliers pride themselves on their variations on classics, such as mellow breakfast blends, stronger after-dinner blends, or those used for espresso. One long-standing combination is Mocha-Java, which combines aroma and strength to make a delicious, potent brew. It takes skill and constant tasting to create and maintain house blends, since even beans from the same place will vary from batch to batch and from year to year.

Since the plant was first cultivated commercially on the continent in the 18th century, the Americas have become the largest producers of coffee in the world. Costa Rican beans are highly prized for their fragrant flavors, balance, and entrancing acidity. Tarrazu is the most famous region, producing excellent coffee, in a land known as the "Switzerland of coffee countries" for its consistency, clean flavors, and attention to detail. This is a good place to source high-altitude beans, such as the high-grade Strictly Hard Bean (SHB).

For a contrast in style, the rugged terrain and remote highlands of Guatemala produce smoky, chocolatey, fruity beans loved for their distinctive individuality. Look out for beans such as those from isolated Huehuetenango, the volcanic slopes above the city of Antigua, and the moist climate of Cobán.

Brazil grows around a third of the world's coffee, much of it on vast plantations stretching in broad sweeps to the horizon. Specialists hunt out high-grade Brazilian coffees, such as those from the older Bourbon plant. Colombia, the second largest coffee producer in the world, is known for the full-bodied, mellow consistency of its washed coffees, from the *supremo* (large) and *excelso* (smaller) beans.

Mexico produces nutty beans with Central American acidity, and is known for its elephantine Maragogype beans. Nicaragua and El Salvador, recovering from political upheaval, are now exporting interesting coffees. Hawaii has the smooth, complex Kona coffees; and Jamaican Blue Mountain is famous for its high-quality beans that command equally high prices.

Africa

Some coffee grows wild in its indigenous landscape of Ethiopia, and the beans produced from this ancient land intrigue drinkers with their winey, gamey, perfumed flavors and aromatic hints of apricots, blueberries, lemon, grapes, and flowers. Look out for coffees such as those from Harrar and from the Sidamo region, which may be labeled after the town of Yirgacheffe. Likely to be grown without pesticides or artificial fertilizers, the natural wildness of these coffee plants translates into the cup as rare, interesting coffees.

Across the Red Sea, Yemeni coffees share some of the same characteristics and may be called Mocha, after the port in Yemen that exported early coffees to Europe. These beans of Arabia can be perfumed with a heavy-bodied piquancy and bright acidity. Dry-processed, they can be earthy with an almost liquorice tang. Mattari and Sanani coffees are the best known.

Grown high up, some at more than 5,000 feet, Kenyan coffees can stop you in your tracks with their pure, fresh, tangy tastes. Kenyan beans are loved for their balance of beautiful body, clean acidity, and berry fruitiness. The top-grade beans are graded AA, and are wet-processed. Kenyan Peaberries, with their single fruit, are a specialty and have a satisfyingly rounded appearance and a smooth, sometimes malty, taste.

Other African countries known for their coffees include Tanzania, Zimbabwe, and Malawi, which can all have the sparkling acidity and fruity flavors of the East African coffee style.

Asia

The Dutch first grew coffee on the Indonesian island of Java, and its name has been used to refer to all the coffees from this country, and, historically, for coffee in general. Javanese coffees are known for their earthy, spicy, rich flavors. Sumatra and Sulawesi also grow luscious, full-bodied coffees with strong, distinctive flavors of herbs, woods, spices, and even syrupy-smooth caramel. Sulawesi coffees are sometimes sold under the former Dutch name for the island, Celebes.

One intriguing, and expensive, Indonesian specialty is Kopi Luak coffee, made from beans eaten and excreted by a small, catlike wild animal, the luak. The beans, transformed in the animal's digestive tract, have,

as you might imagine, something of a cult following. Some Indonesian coffees are aged to mimic the taste acquired when the beans were stockpiled in this damp, warm climate or underwent long sea voyages to the West. Neighboring Papua New Guinea produces coffees with a perfumed tropical fruitiness.

Coffee has been grown in India since as early as the 17th century, and specialties include aged Monsoon coffees, where the beans are exposed to the monsoon winds in open warehouses; the result is a coffee with a special, mellow flavor. Southern India grows other coffees with enticing scents of spices. Mysore coffees are one variety known for quality, since they come from a state where arabica plants are grown.

flavored and decaf

Certain flavors such as vanilla and chocolate have an affinity with coffee, hence the chocolate on the top of a cappuccino, or the delicious addition of a spoonful of vanilla sugar to an after-dinner cup. Spiced coffees are a traditional brew in the Middle East, where the grounds may be mixed with cardamom and other flavors, like cinnamon, nutmeg, and cloves. On parts of the Amalfi coast in Italy, they sometimes add a twist of peel from their famous lemons, and the habit has followed some of the Italians living in America. Modern flavored coffees use essential oils and other flavorings to make such brews as tiramisu, pecan, and raspberries and cream. You can also buy or make flavored sugar syrups to add to brewed coffees (orange is a good one), or add a dash of a liqueur for an extra tasty kick.

Decaffeinated coffees are made by dissolving the caffeine out of the bean using chemical solvents or water. Look for decaf sold by people who care about quality. Some of the taste disappears with the caffeine, so you need coffee made from beans with plenty of flavor in the first place. Some suppliers use cheap, less-delicious beans to compensate for the cost of the decaffeination process, and this is one reason why the drink can taste underpowered in more than one sense. Robusta coffees, incidentally, have about twice as much caffeine in them as the higher-quality arabicas.

Whether you like the short, black blast of espresso, the clean smoothness of filter coffee, or milky sips of cappuccino, this section guides you through the practicalities of making coffee, from shopping to sipping, and looks at how its flavors can be used in food.

the brew

buying and storing

Coffee becomes infinitely more appealing and interesting if you buy from a specialized supplier. You can purchase through the internet and by mail order, or steep yourself in the sensory delight of the store itself with all the entrancing aromas and busy sounds: the grinding, the chinking, the shake, rattle, and roll of the beans. A good retailer will have an interesting choice of high-quality beans; they may well do their own roasting, or get a good roaster to do it to their specification, and will be able to give you advice on what to try, so expanding your enjoyment to a wider range of tastes.

Freshness is the key to good coffee. The aromatic oils start to disappear immediately after roasting, so it is best to buy smaller amounts of freshly roasted coffee regularly, instead of a large amount in one trip. Buy your coffee as you would other fresh foods, and use it at its peak. When beans are freshly roasted, the grounds tend to foam up when you add water.

Ideally, buy whole beans and grind them at home, because the oils lose their volatile aromas even more quickly once the coffee is ground. A good retailer will grind the beans for you, but, best of all, do it yourself, just before brewing. An inexpensive propeller-blade grinder is a good way to start, or pay more for a grinder that mills the coffee between disks to get a more even grind, and has settings that can be adjusted for different grades, from coarse to fine.

Coffee should be stored in an airtight, dry container, in a cool cabinet rather than the refrigerator. You can also freeze beans in an air-tight bag for a couple of months, and grind them while still frozen.

secrets for the perfect cup

Making coffee correctly allows you to really taste the full, fresh, and interesting flavors on offer. These four straightforward principles make all the difference between insipid meekness or brutish bitterness, and aromatic energy.

• Buy freshly roasted, good-quality whole beans and grind them just before brewing.

• The grind should be right for whatever method you are using (espresso, plunge-pot, filter, or otherwise—see pages 38–41).

• Measure the amount of coffee and water used, and the length of time the coffee brews. Getting the proper proportion of coffee to water and letting them brew together for the right amount of time means you extract the most character and aromatic oils from the beans without the brew becoming bitter. If you want weaker coffee, it is better to add hot water to properly brewed coffee than to use too much water or too few beans.

• With the exception of Middle Eastern coffee (which is boiled), pour the water onto the grounds when it has just boiled. This dissolves the soluble flavors from the coffee without scalding the subtleties into bitterness. Do not keep coffee warm on the heat, or it will become bitter and stewed.

The following pages outline the various methods of making the perfect cup, so you can be sure to get the right pressure in your espresso machine and the perfect froth on your cappuccino.

espresso know-how

Espresso works on the principle of forcing hot water through finely ground, dark-roasted coffee under pressure so that it blasts through the grounds, extracting the maximum flavor. The water emulsifies with the oils from the beans to make a drink that is lusciously full-bodied and rich in flavor.

At home, Italians tend to make stove-top espressos. The Moka stove-top is the classic model, and there are now many others available. These pots are designed to brew a particular amount of coffee and range in size from those for a couple of cups to larger pots for more people. Fill the bottom half with water up to the rivet on the side and fill the coffee container up to the brim with finely ground coffee, leveling it off gently without compressing it, or the water will not be able to get through evenly. Screw the top part onto the bottom as tightly as possible to prevent leakage. When the coffee is ready, you will hear the bubbling, breathy "ploff-ploff-ploff" of air being forced through the connecting tube, once all the water has gone through.

If you want to buy a home espresso machine, try to find one that provides high pressure, such as the pump-action models, which get more flavor from the coffee. The more expensive machines get closer to the sophisticated engineering of the professional models in cafés. You can buy machines with convenient little ready-to-use pods of ground coffee, but this restricts your choice, and the beans will not be freshly ground.

filters to French presses

Each of these methods requires 2 tablespoons of coffee per
¾ cup of water and need to brew for around four to six minutes
to extract the fullest flavor from the beans.

• The most primitive method is to put coarsely ground coffee in
a pitcher, pour in the hot water, give the mixture a stir, and leave
to infuse for about five or six minutes. You can wrap the pot in a
dishtowel and put a saucer on top to retain the heat and aromas.

• The plunge-pot, French press, or cafetière, produces coffee full of the luscious aromatic oils of the coffee bean. Use coarsely ground coffee and give the coffee a stir once you have poured on the water. Infuse for four minutes. Again, you can wrap a dishtowel around the pot to keep the liquid hot while it brews, or use an insulated plunge-pot.

• When making filter coffee, wet the medium-fine ground coffee first with a little hot water to help the water filter through evenly. If you are making filter coffee by hand rather than in a machine, add the water slowly to allow it to extract the flavor from the beans. This should take about four minutes. Give the coffee a stir before serving, so the flavors of the brew are equally dispersed.

• Old-fashioned French drip pots work on the same principle as filter coffee and come in three parts: a pot, a filter with holes, and a top section with a lid. You put medium-ground coffee in the filter, pour water into the top part, and let it drip through to the bottom.

• Recently revived, the vacuum-pot method requires a medium-fine grind and produces coffee with a beautiful clarity of flavor.

milk and sugar?

Milk goes with coffee in many different and delicious ways. The main principle is that hot milk works better than cold. For this reason, French waiters simultaneously pour a black jet of coffee from one pot and hot milk from another to form a *café au lait*, and an Italian "stains" an espresso with a drop of steamed milk to make a *caffè macchiato* or adds it, half and half, to make a latte.

Milk softens and alters flavors. When trying a new kind of bean, taste the drink first without milk to get a better grasp of its subtleties, then add the milk and taste once more to judge how its character is altered.

Steamed, frothy milk floats on the top of the cup, giving a combination of black silk and white velvet in each sip. Cream is another way to add a seductive layer of smoothness to your cup.

Sugar takes away some of the bitterness in coffee, though well-made coffee has a subtle, glancing, alert edge of bitterness and does not call for sweetness in the same way as a brutish, stewed brew. Some like to add a spoonful to dark-roasted coffee, such as espresso, but not to lighter styles. Eating little pastries or sugared cookies with your coffee is, of course, another excellent way to sweeten the moment.

cappuccino, latte, and au lait ...

The classic cappuccino is made using one third espresso, one third steamed milk, and one third foam. Espresso machines usually have a metal wand that steams and froths the milk. You can also buy little electric gadgets that quickly whisk up hot milk so it doubles or trebles in volume. Alternatively, heat milk in a saucepan or microwave and then whisk by hand until it froths. You can buy special milk-frothing whisks. Some of these come with containers you can put in the microwave to heat up the milk. Pour the hot milk onto the coffee, holding back the froth with a spoon, and add the frothed milk last. If desired, top off the cappuccino with powdered chocolate.

You can also drink a *cappuccino senza schiuma* (without foam) or a *cappuccino chiaro*, with less coffee and more milk, or the darker *cappuccino scuro*, with less milk. Just use your eye and your tastebuds to judge the proportions.

A caffè latte is roughly half hot or steamed milk and half espresso mixed together. The French *café au lait* is the same, but made with filter coffee.

coffee drinking and café society

From the breakfast wake-up jolt to the after-dinner digestive, coffee is consumed all around the world, morning, noon, and night. There are many reasons for coffee's widespread popularity, from the medical to the gastronomic. But whether it is drunk by Bedouin tribesmen around a fire or by city office workers grabbing a cardboard cup between meetings, at base coffee's appeal comes from being a source of energy. Weight for weight, there is less caffeine in coffee than in tea; but cup for cup, coffee wins the race. Caffeine is quickly absorbed into your bloodstream and provides a stretch of mental alertness and focus that makes you feel as efficiently active and ready to rev as a well-oiled engine.

Each country has evolved different places where people can drink, meet, and take a break, from the zinc-topped counters of French cafés and the wood-paneled, well-worn sophistication of the Viennese coffeehouse, to the fast, bright zap of the modern coffee chain. Café society is about people meeting, thinking, writing, talking, and watching—or simply sitting in amiable surroundings with the company of a cup of coffee and a slice of cake, taking time out, in sips.

coffee and cream cheesecake

This cheesecake, with its glossy white top, shows off the classic combination of coffee and cream.

7 oz. graham crackers, about 11

6 tablespoons butter

1 tablespoon sugar

Coffee filling

2 tablespoons ground coffee

1 lb. cream cheese

4 egg yolks

1 cup sugar

⅔ cup heavy cream

1 vanilla bean

2 egg whites

Topping

1½ cups sour cream

a springform cake pan, 8 inches diameter, lightly greased with butter

a baking tray

serves 8–10

To make the crust, put the crackers into a plastic bag and crush them finely with a rolling pin. Melt the butter in a saucepan, then stir in the crushed crackers and sugar. Press the mixture into the bottom of the prepared cake pan, then press it evenly about 2 inches up the sides. Bake in a preheated oven at 400°F for 10 minutes, then remove from the oven and let cool. Reduce the oven temperature to 325°F.

Meanwhile, to make the coffee filling, put the ground coffee in a measuring cup, add ⅔ cup boiling water, and let cool.

Put the cream cheese into a bowl and stir so it loosens slightly. Stir in the egg yolks, one at a time, then the sugar, then the cream. Slit the vanilla bean down one side and, using a teaspoon or knife, scrape out the seeds into the cream cheese mixture and stir well. Stir ½ cup of the cooled coffee into the mixture.

Put the egg whites in a clean, greasefree bowl and beat until soft peaks form. Fold into the cream cheese mixture, then spoon into the prepared cake pan and put on the baking tray. Bake at 325°F for 1 hour. Leave, with the oven turned off and the door closed, for another 30 minutes. Remove from the oven and transfer to a wire rack. Reheat the oven to 425°F.

To make the topping, put the sour cream into a bowl and stir to loosen. Spoon over the cheesecake, spreading it out with a spatula to get a smooth, even layer. Cook in the reheated oven for 6–7 minutes, to set the sour cream (it will form a white, glossy topping that contrasts nicely with the pale, coffee-colored cheesecake).

Remove from the oven and let cool. Run a knife around the outside of the cheesecake, then unclip the pan (it is important to run the knife around the cheesecake, or you risk splitting it when you release the spring). Serve with coffee.

Italian coffee drinking

Hot shots of coffee fuel the animated Italians. It seems to suit their speed and spirit: even the buzzing Vespas seem to run on espresso. All through the day, you see people stopping off to stand at a bar for *un caffè* (an espresso) to recharge their batteries and go, go, go again.

The cappuccino is a milky breakfast brew that may be drunk with a *cornetto* (a croissant) or another pastry. The drink—with its hood of steamed, frothed milk—is named after the color of the habit of the Capuchin monks, who, in turn, were named after the hoods (*cappuccio*) of their habits.

The classic espresso is a very short measure—just a few long, deliciously bitter sips—and a well-made one has a pale brown foam, or *crema*, on top. A double espresso (*caffè doppio*) is a double measure. A *caffè lungo* has more water for a less strong drink, and a *caffè ristretto* has less water for a stronger brew. A *caffè macchiato* has a dollop of steamed milk, while a *latte macchiato* is milk with a drop of coffee.

On hot days, you can refresh yourself with a *caffè freddo* or iced coffee, or make that a *caffè latte freddo* with the addition of milk. And on a cold day or after a meal, you could add a drop of liquor for a fortifying, warming *caffè corretto*.

Don't toast all the almonds—reserve a few untoasted to use as a pale decoration on the brown ice cream. Alternatively, cut some of the toasted almonds into thin shards to sprinkle over each serving.

coffee and almond ice cream

1¼ cups heavy cream

1¼ cups whole milk

3 tablespoons coarsely ground coffee (grind for 8–12 seconds)

1 cup slivered almonds, plus 2 tablespoons for decoration (optional)

4 extra-large egg yolks

3½ tablespoons sugar

a baking tray

an ice-cream maker or freezer trays

serves 4–6

Put the cream and milk into a heavy saucepan. Add the coffee and stir over low heat for 5 minutes, without boiling, to infuse the flavors. Remove from the heat and let cool for 10 minutes, then pour the mixture through a strainer lined with damp cheesecloth into a bowl.

Put the almonds on the baking tray and toast them in a preheated oven at 400°F, checking after a couple of minutes and giving them a shake. The nuts are ready when they are pale brown and smell sweet and toasty.

Put the egg yolks and sugar into a heatproof bowl and beat well. Reheat the coffee cream, without boiling, then beat it into the eggs, a little at a time.

Put the bowl over a saucepan of simmering water and stir constantly with a wooden spoon until the mixture thickens slightly (it will thicken more as it cools). You can also do this in a heavy saucepan directly over very low heat. (If the mixture curdles, strain it to remove the strands of solidified egg.) Stir in the toasted almonds.

Remove from the heat and cool the mixture by putting the bowl into a larger bowl of cold water. When cool, chill in the refrigerator until quite cold. Churn in an ice-cream maker, according to the manufacturer's instructions. Alternatively, partly freeze the mixture in shallow trays, then remove and beat to break down the ice crystals. Partly freeze and beat again—the more you do this, the smoother the ice cream will be. Freeze until solid.

Serve plain, or topped with the reserved almonds, if using.

mocha truffle tart

Serve this intensely flavored tart slightly warm from the oven.

4 heaping tablespoons
all-purpose flour

1 tablespoon unsweetened
cocoa powder

2 tablespoons sugar

4 tablespoons unsalted butter,
cut into small pieces

1 extra-large egg yolk, beaten

sour cream or crème
fraîche, to serve

coffee and chocolate filling

8 oz. bittersweet chocolate,
chopped

3 teaspoons instant
espresso powder

3 extra-large egg yolks

1 extra-large whole egg

1½ heaping tablespoons sugar

*a loose-bottom tart pan,
9 inches diameter*

foil and baking beans or rice

serves 6

To make the dough, sift the flour, cocoa, and sugar into a bowl. Add the pieces of butter and, using your fingertips, rub them into the dry ingredients until the mixture looks like bread crumbs. Add 1 tablespoon water and the beaten egg yolk. Stir the mixture with a knife, then, using your fingertips, gently draw it together into a ball. Chill for at least 1 hour.

Transfer the chilled dough to a floured work surface and roll out as thinly as possible. Drape the dough over the rolling pin, then drape it over the prepared tart pan. Press it into the corners of the pan, then trim the edges of the dough and flute it with your fingers. Chill for at least 30 minutes.

Remove from the refrigerator and line with foil, then fill with baking beans or rice. Bake in a preheated oven at 350°F for 20 minutes, then remove the beans and foil, and return the pie crust to the oven for another 5 minutes to dry out the base. This is called "baking blind." Remove from the oven and keep the oven at the same temperature.

Meanwhile, to make the filling, put the chocolate into a heatproof bowl set over a saucepan of gently simmering water (do not let any water or steam touch the chocolate or it will be spoiled). Stir in the espresso powder.

Put the egg yolks, whole egg, and sugar into a bowl and, using electric beaters or a wire whisk, beat until light, fluffy, and doubled in volume. Stir in the chocolate and coffee mixture, then pour into the pie crust. This mixture sets like lava, with every bump and ridge in evidence, so if you want an even appearance, use a knife dipped in hot water to smooth the top.

Bake for 15 minutes (no longer, or it will dry out). Serve warm, with a dollop of sour cream or crème fraîche.

These "kisses" are delicate walnut and coffee cookies joined
with a rich chocolate-coffee ganache.

walnut coffee kisses

⅓ cup walnuts

I stick unsalted butter

4½ tablespoons caster sugar

½ beaten egg

¾ cup self-rising flour

I teaspoon instant
espresso powder

Ganache

4 oz. bittersweet chocolate

4 tablespoons unsalted butter

½ cup heavy cream

1½ teaspoons instant
espresso powder

*2 baking trays covered with
nonstick parchment paper*

makes 24 cookies, 12 "kisses"

Heat oven to 350°F. Finely chop the walnuts—this is best done with a knife to prevent the nuts becoming oily.

Put the butter and sugar into a bowl and beat until creamy. Stir in the beaten egg, then fold in the sifted flour. Stir in the espresso power, then the chopped walnuts. Put an even number (about 24) tablespoons of the mixture onto baking trays covered with nonstick parchment paper. Bake for about 10 minutes, or until light brown around the edges. Remove from the oven and let cool and firm up on the tray for a couple of minutes. Carefully transfer to a wire rack to cool completely.

Meanwhile, to make the ganache, break the chocolate into pieces and put in a saucepan. Add butter and cream and heat without boiling, until the butter melts. Beat in the espresso powder. Remove from the heat and stir. The mixture will thicken as it cools. Carefully sandwich the cool, fragile cookies together with the ganache.

Middle Eastern coffee

An *ibrik*, or *kanaka*, is the tapered pot with a long handle and a pouring lip used in the Middle Eastern method of boiling coffee with water. Mix one or two heaping teaspoons of very finely ground coffee with an equal amount of sugar for each demitasse (little cup) of water. The *ibrik* must be only half full as the mixture will expand as it boils. Bring to a boil over medium heat, then reduce the heat to low. Bring to a boil again, then either turn the heat off, or repeat the boiling once more.

Half-fill the cups with coffee, then add some of the prized foam to the top of each drink. For an extra-aromatic brew, use Middle Eastern coffee that is ready-mixed with cardamom.

spiced orange coffee syrup

A syrup for ice cream spiced with the cardamom that often flavors Middle Eastern coffee.

10 green cardamom pods
1¼ cups sugar
½ cup strong coffee or espresso
1 teaspoon finely grated orange zest
1 cinnamon stick, broken into pieces

serves 6–8

Crush the cardamom pods with a knife and scrape out the seeds. Put the sugar into a heavy saucepan, add ¼ cup water, and heat very slowly until the sugar dissolves—gently draw a spoon across the sugar to help the process. When all the sugar has dissolved, boil for 2 minutes, then stir in the coffee, orange zest, cinnamon, and cardamom. Let it cool so the flavors infuse, then strain and store the syrup in an airtight container in the refrigerator.

To serve, pour onto vanilla or chocolate ice cream.

coffee and alcohol

Coffee is often served at the end of a meal and it combines beautifully with liqueurs, enjoyed either alongside one another, or in the same cup. To make a classic Irish coffee, pour Irish whiskey (other liquor works well, too) into a glass with a spoonful of sugar; add strong, hot coffee, and pour heavy cream over the back of a spoon so it floats on top. Alternatively, simply add a drop of brandy, Calvados, grappa, or any number of liqueurs for an extra glow of heat to black or white coffee. Rum and orange-flavored liqueur such as Cointreau work particularly well.

iced coffee

You can add a splash of a liqueur such as Cointreau or rum to this deliciously refreshing drink.

For each person
2 tablespoons ground coffee
4 ice cubes
**I small scoop vanilla or chocolate
ice cream (optional)**
½ cup milk
I teaspoon sugar, or to taste
a dash of liqueur (optional)

serves 1

Make the coffee using your regular method, but make it stronger than usual (2 tablespoons ground coffee to ½ cup water) because it will be diluted by the ice. When brewed, pour the coffee onto the ice cubes. As an extra touch, you can put a scoop of ice cream on the ice cubes before you pour in the coffee. Stir in the milk, sugar, and liqueur, if using. Serve immediately or chill until required.

credits and resources

ALLEGRO COFFEE COMPANY
1930 Central Avenue
Boulder CO
(800) 666 4869
www.allegro-coffee.com

ANCORA COFFEE ROASTERS
931 East Main Street
Madison WI 53703
(800) 260 0217
www.ancora-coffee.com

CAFFE APPASSIONATO
311 Walnut Street
Newtonville MA 02460
(617) 332 6886
www.appassionatocoffee.com

THE COFFEE MILL ROASTERY
161 East Franklin Street
Chapel Hill NC 27514
(919) 929 1727
www.coffeeroastery.com

DAYBREAK COFFEE ROASTERS
2377 Main Street
Glastonbury CT 06033
(800) 882 5282
www.daybreakcoffee.com

DISTANT LANDS COFFEE ROASTERS
13081 State Hwy 64 West
Tyler TX 75704-9493
(800) 346 5459
www.dlcoffee.com

GRAFFEO COFFEE ROASTING COMPANY
735 Colombus Avenue
San Fransiso CA 94133
(800) 222 6250
www.graffeo.com

GREEN MOUNTAIN COFFEE ROASTERS
33 Coffee Lane
Waterbury VT 05676
(800) 223 6768
www.gmcr.com

GREENE BROTHERS SPECIALITY COFFEE
ROASTERS
313 High Street
Hackettstown NJ 07840
(888) 665 2626

H. R. HIGGINS (COFFEE-MAN) LTD
79 Duke St
London W1K 5AS, UK
Tel +44 20 7629 3913
enquiries@hrhiggins.co.uk
www.hrhiggins.co.uk

WWW.INEEDCOFFEE.COM

JAVA GOURMET.COM
21946 Panama Drive
Golden CO 80401
(303) 884 0026
www.javagourmet.com

LAYTON FERN & CO. LTD
27 Rathbone Place
London W1P 2EP, UK
Tel +44 20 7636 2237
sales@laytonfern.fsnet.co.uk
www.coffeeisferns.co.uk

MCNULTY'S TEA AND COFFEE
109 Christopher Street
New York NY 10014
(212) 242 5351
(800) 356-5200
www.mcnultys.com

MONMOUTH COFFEE COMPANY
27 Monmouth St
London WC2H 9DD, UK
Tel +44 20 7379 3516
2 Park Street
London SE1 9AB, UK
Tel +44 20 7645 3585
coffee@monmouthcoffee.co.uk

THE ORIGINAL SAN JUAN COFFEE
ROASTING COMPANY
18 Cannery Landing
Friday Harbor WA 98250
(800) 624 4119

OZZIES COFFEE AND TEA
57 Seventh Avenue
Brooklyn NY 11215
(718) 768 6695
and
249 5th Avenue
Brooklyn NY11215
(718) 768 6868
www.ozziescoffee.com

PEET'S COFFEE AND TEA
PO Box 12509
Berkeley CA 94712-3509
(510) 594 2100
www.peets.com

ROYAL BLEND COFFEE COMPANY
PO Box 7066
Bend OR 97708
(800) 742 2690
www.royalblend.com

URTH CAFFE
8565 Melrose Ave
West Hollywood CA 90069
(310) 253 7788
www.urthcaffe.com

WILDERNESS COFFEE COMPANY
13541 Grove Drive North
Maple Grove MN 55369
(763) 420 4830
www.wilderness.safeshopper.com

FAIR TRADE ORGANIZATIONS

The Fair Trade principle is a
commitment to setting new
standards for commercial trading
in developing countries.

EQUAL EXCHANGE
251 Revere Street
Canton MA 02021
(781) 830 0303
www.equalexchange.com

CAFÉDIRECT AND TEADIRECT
City Cloisters
Suite B2, 196 Old Street
London EC1V 9FR , UK
020 7490 9520
www.cafedirect.co.uk

TRANSFAIR
1611 Telegraph Avenue , Suite 900
Oakland CA 94612
(510) 663 5260
www.transfairusa.org

PICTURE CREDITS

Page 6, below right: Washing coffee
cherries, Cocla co-operative, Peru /
ph Richard Hide © Cafédirect.

index

acknowledgments

I'd like to thank everyone I have talked to about coffee, particularly Tony Higgins of the excellent H. R. Higgins coffee and tea shop near Oxford Circus in London, and David and Liz Phillips, the very knowledgeable owners of The Steamer Trading Cookshop in Lewes (+44 1273 487230) and Alfriston (+44 1323 870055), East Sussex, UK. The Monmouth Coffee Company in Covent Garden and Borough Market, London, has always inspired me to explore coffees from all around the world, and, along with Higgins', also a very good shop, features in the photographs in the book. Many thanks to the Fair Trade organization Cafédirect for images. At Ryland Peters & Small, a big thank you to Alison Starling, Sophie Bevan, Luis Peral-Aranda, Gabriella La Grazie; and to Emily Chalmers and Debi Treloar for making the pictures so beautiful yet drinkably real. Thanks, in general, to my aunt Julia Ellis for bringing me packets and tales from her travels, and to Gail and Frances for book hunting.

PUBLISHER'S ACKNOWLEDGMENTS: The publisher would like to thank the Monmouth Coffee Company, H. R. Higgins (Coffee-Man) Ltd, and Layton Fern & Co. Ltd for allowing us to photograph in their premises. Thanks also to Cafédirect for the loan of images. cafédirect